FRENCH
STAND UP AND COOK BOOK

Beryl Frank

CROWN PUBLISHERS, INC.   NEW YORK, N.Y.

Library of Congress catalog card number: 78-74614
ISBN: 0-517-535718
Copyright © 1979 by Ottenheimer Publishers, Inc.
Printed in the United States of America.

Contents

Introduction

The great talent of a truly good French chef is his ability to improvise. Chicken Marengo was created for Napoleon after the French defeat of the Austrians at Marengo. The dish was created by a talented chef who used the available provisions plus brandy to create a culinary masterpiece. Napoleon and many generations since have enjoyed this dish.

Food is a pleasurable experience to the French cook. It must be a good taste experience and be pleasing to the eye as well. Eye-appeal is almost as important as good taste for the French cook. Most dishes, from appetizers to desserts, are decoratively garnished. There are many examples of this in the recipes included here.

Butter is considered by many to be a must for French cooking. The French use unsweetened butter. If, however, because of a special diet, you cannot use butter, margarine is a very adequate substitute for the recipes in this book.

Most important of all to the person who wants to search for new cooking experiences in the French manner is the trying of new recipes. Let your own common sense as well as your personal taste guide you to making a change that suits your own palate in any given recipe. The truly gifted cook will enjoy making culinary discoveries from new recipes. Include taste treats in your daily cooking and you, too, may change a plain ordinary pancake into a thin delicious crepe. Bon apetit!

Brandy Pâté

½ pound chicken livers
2 tablespoons butter
1 small onion, chopped
  fine
¼ teaspoon thyme
1 small bay leaf
2 ounces chopped
  mushrooms
3 strips crisp bacon,
  chopped

⅓ cup cream
1 tablespoon port
1 tablespoon dry sherry
1 teaspoon brandy
2 teaspoons salt
1 teaspoon pepper
2 tablespoons melted
  butter

Clean and dry chicken livers.

Melt 2 tablespoons butter in pan. Sauté livers, onion, thyme, bay leaf, mushrooms, and chopped bacon 7 to 10 minutes. Remove from heat; discard bay leaf. Blend mixture with cream until smooth. (A blender makes this very easy.) Push through sieve or food mill into bowl. Stir in port, sherry, and brandy; season with salt and pepper. Spoon mixture into serving dish. Cover pâté with melted butter. Refrigerate until butter is firm on top. This helps keep the pâté moist and looks attractive.

Serve pâté with hot toast points or your favorite crackers. Makes about 1½ cups of pâté.

Curried Pâté

¼ pound butter
1 medium onion, finely chopped
2 strips crisp cooked bacon
1 pound chicken livers
1 chicken-stock cube

2 hard-boiled eggs
1 teaspoon salt
½ teaspoon pepper
1½ teaspoons curry powder
2 tablespoons dry sherry
½ cup cream

Melt butter. Gently sauté onion and bacon until onion is transparent.

Wash chicken livers. Add to pan with crumbled stock cube; cook for 5 to 7 minutes or until livers are cooked through. Remove from heat; allow to cool slightly. Add roughly chopped eggs, salt, pepper, curry powder, sherry, and cream to livers. Puree (in blender) until smooth, then push through food mill or sieve.

Grease 10 x 3-inch mold. Refrigerate pâté in mold until firm.

Unmold pâté carefully onto platter. Surround with small toast points or your favorite crackers. Makes 6 to 8 servings.

Ham Pâté

6 tablespoons butter
1 small onion, grated
½ teaspoon dried basil
¼ teaspoon freshly
   ground pepper
¾ cup dry white wine
2 tablespoons brandy
1 pound chicken livers,
   cleaned and halved

¾ cup cream
4 ounces sliced ham,
   chopped fine
3 ounces ham fat,
   chopped fine
1 tablespoon finely
   chopped parsley
1 teaspoon salt

Melt 4 tablespoons butter in large skillet. Add onion, basil, and pepper. Sauté until onion is soft. Add wine and brandy; simmer, uncovered, until liquid is reduced by half. Add chicken livers; simmer for 5 minutes or until livers are just cooked. Remove livers from pan; place in blender.

Bring remaining liquid to boil; boil, uncovered, until ½ cup liquid remains. Add liquid and cream to chicken livers; blend on medium speed. Push through sieve or food mill.

Melt 2 tablespoons butter in skillet with ham and ham fat; sauté together about 2 minutes. Add this mixture and parsley to chicken livers. Mix well; season with salt. Pour into serving dish; refrigerate until firm.

Serve pâté chilled. Makes 6 to 8 servings.

Salmon Pâté

1 tablespoon unflavored
  gelatin
½ cup hot water
1 chicken-stock cube
1 8-ounce can red salmon
¼ cup mayonnaise
2 tablespoons chopped
  parsley

2 teaspoons lemon juice
2 shallots or spring
  onions, roughly
  chopped
½ cup cream
1 teaspoon salt
Dash of pepper

Put gelatin, hot water, and chicken-stock cube into electric blender. Blend at high speed 2 minutes. Add undrained salmon and remaining ingredients; blend until smooth. Pour mixture into lightly greased individual molds; refrigerate until set. Unmold onto leaves of crisp lettuce. Serve with Green Horseradish Sauce. Makes 4 servings.

Green Horseradish Sauce

1 egg
1 egg yolk
1 teaspoon prepared
  mustard
½ cup chopped parsley
1 tablespoon white vinegar

Salt and pepper to taste
1 cup oil
1 tablespoon bottled
  horseradish relish

Put 1 whole egg, egg yolk, mustard, parsley, vinegar, salt, and pepper into electric blender; blend for 1 minute. Gradually add oil until approximately ½ cup oil has been added and mixture has thickened. Slowly pour in remaining oil. Mixture will thicken as oil is added. Add horseradish; blend a few seconds more. Refrigerate before serving. Spoon over the Salmon Pâté.

Quiche Lorraine

Quiche is delicious served warm or cold, cut into either slices or squares.

Pastry

1¼ cups plain flour
Pinch of salt

6 tablespoons butter
1 tablespoon water

Sift flour and salt into bowl. Cut in butter until mixture resembles fine bread crumbs. Add water (more than 1 tablespoon if needed) to make a soft dough. Turn pastry onto lightly floured surface. Knead lightly; roll out to fit base and sides of 9-inch pie pan or a rectangular pan of your choice. Press pastry into pan. Refrigerate at least 30 minutes.

Filling

**¼ pound bacon, cut into
  small pieces**
**1 medium onion, finely
  chopped**
**½ cup grated Gruyère
  cheese**

3 eggs
½ cup cream
¾ cup milk
**Pinch each of salt,
  pepper, and nutmeg**

Stir bacon and onion in skillet over low heat until bacon is crisp and onion transparent. Drain; allow to cool. Spread over bottom of pastry. Sprinkle grated cheese over bacon.

Beat eggs, cream, and milk together with seasonings; spoon carefully over cheese. Bake at 450°F for 10 minutes. Reduce temperature to 300°F; bake for 20 to 25 minutes more. Makes 6 to 8 servings.

Avocado Cream Soup

1¼ cups chicken stock
2 ripe avocados
¾ cup cream
½ cup milk
1 teaspoon salt
Dash of freshly ground pepper

Place chicken stock in bowl; set aside.

Peel avocados; remove seeds. Put chopped avocados in blender with cream and milk. Blend on medium speed until smooth. (If you do not have a blender, press avocado into a paste with a fork, then blend with cream and milk.) Put this mixture in with chicken stock; stir until smooth. (For an even finer consistency, press through a sieve.) Season with salt and pepper. Refrigerate until well-chilled.

Spoon soup into bowls and enjoy. Makes 4 servings.

French Onion Soup

4 tablespoons butter
4 large onions, peeled and sliced
1 teaspoon sugar
2 teaspoons flour
2 15-ounce cans beef consommé
3 cups water
¼ teaspoon pepper
8 slices white bread
8 ounces grated cheddar cheese
2 ounces grated Parmesan cheese

Heat butter in large saucepan. Add onions; sauté until onions are tender and golden brown. Add sugar and flour. Stir in consommé and water; bring to boil. Reduce heat; simmer, covered, for 30 minutes. Season with pepper.

Cut bread slices into 4-inch rounds. Toast the rounds.

Combine grated cheeses. Cover bread with cheese mixture. Grill under broiler until cheese is golden brown.

Put 1 cheese slice into each soup bowl; pour hot soup over it. Serve at once. Makes 8 or more servings.

Pumpkin Vichyssoise

1½ pounds canned pumpkin
2 leeks or large onions, sliced or chopped
¾ pound potatoes, diced
4 cups chicken stock
1¼ cups cream
1 teaspoon salt
Dash of pepper

Place pumpkin, leeks, potatoes, and chicken stock into large saucepan. Bring to boil; simmer, uncovered, for 25 minutes or until potatoes are very soft and tender. Put vegetables and liquid through sieve to make fine puree. Return to pan. Add cream, salt, and pepper; again bring to boil. Stir soup over low flame; simmer for 5 minutes more. This may be served hot but is usually served chilled. Makes 4 to 6 servings.

Boeuf Bourguignonne

3 pounds round steak,
  cut into 1-inch cubes
4 strips bacon
12 small onions, peeled
  whole
¼ cup or more flour
1 teaspoon salt
½ teaspoon pepper
2 tablespoons butter
2 tablespoons oil
2 carrots, sliced

1 clove garlic, crushed
½ pound button
  mushrooms
1 cup red wine
1 cup beef stock
1 teaspoon thyme
2 teaspoons sugar
1 tablespoon tomato
  paste
1 bay leaf

Trim meat into 1-inch cubes. Cut bacon into pieces. Peel onions. Coat meat in flour seasoned with salt and pepper.

Heat butter and oil in large shallow pan. Brown the steak cubes well on all sides; remove from pan.

Add onions to pan. Cook until lightly browned. Remove; set aside.

Add bacon, carrots, garlic, and mushrooms to pan. Cook slowly, stirring occasionally, until bacon is crisp. Add wine, beef stock, and rest of ingredients except onions; bring to boil. Add meat to sauce. After all is heated through, transfer to ovenproof baking dish; cover. Bake at 350°F for 1 hour. Add onions; cook for 1 hour more, until meat is tender to the fork. Remove bay leaf before serving. Makes 4 to 6 servings.

Beef Cubes in Sherry

Delicious!

2 tablespoons shortening
2 pounds lean stewing beef, cubed
1 package onion-soup mix
1 cup sherry wine
1 can cream of mushroom soup
1 teaspoon garlic salt
¼ pound sliced mushrooms

Heat shortening in heavy pot. Brown the beef cubes on all sides. Add remaining ingredients in order given; stir well. Cover pot; simmer mixture at least 1 hour or until meat is tender to the fork. Add additional water or soup stock as needed.

Serve beef over broad noodles. Makes 4 to 6 servings.

Stuffed Fillet of Beef

1½ **pounds fillet steak**

Chicken Stuffing

2 **tablespoons butter**
1 **onion, chopped fine**
2 **strips bacon**
1 **chicken breast**
Enough water to cover
   chicken
1 **egg**
2 **tablespoons fresh**
   bread crumbs

2 **tablespoons chopped**
   parsley
1 **teaspoon salt**
¼ **teaspoon pepper**

8 **ounces button**
   mushrooms, sliced thin
½ **cup dry red wine**

Using small, sharp knife, cut a pocket in middle of fillet. Cut almost to edges; do not cut through. Set aside.

Melt butter; sauté onion and bacon over low heat until golden brown.

In another pan cover chicken breast with water. Bring to boil; simmer for 25 minutes, until chicken is tender. Drain. Remove meat from bones; remove skin; chop chicken meat fine. Add chicken to bacon and onion mixture. Add egg, bread crumbs, parsley, salt, and pepper; mix well. Press chicken stuffing firmly into pocket of steak.

Place meat into greased baking dish. Bake at 350°F 40 minutes (a little less if you prefer rare meat). Surround meat with mushrooms; stir to mix in pan juices. Cook 10 minutes more. Pour wine over meat; bake another 5 minutes. To serve, slice meat and arrange it on a platter. Pour mushroom sauce over meat. Makes 4 servings.

Beef Stew in Red Wine

2 pounds lean stew meat,
   cubed
1¾ cups water
1 teaspoon salt
½ teaspoon freshly
   ground pepper
1 bay leaf
½ cup tomato paste
1 cup dry red wine
3 carrots, peeled and
   sliced

12 small onions, peeled
4 ounces sliced
   mushrooms
2 tablespoons butter
¼ cup flour
Salt and pepper to taste
Chopped parsley for
   garnish

Place cubed meat, 1¼ cups water, 1 teaspoon salt, pepper, and bay leaf into large pan. Bring to boil; reduce heat. Cover; simmer gently 1½ hours. Add tomato paste, red wine, carrots, onions, and mushrooms; simmer at least 30 minutes more or until vegetables are tender. Remove vegetables and meat from pan, reserving the liquid.

Melt butter in separate saucepan; stir in flour over low heat about 1 minute. Remove from heat; stir in reserved liquid and ½ cup water. Return to heat; stir until sauce thickens, about 2 minutes. Replace meat and vegetables into pan; season with salt and pepper. Gently reheat the now- completed stew.

Serve stew garnished with chopped parsley. Makes 4 to 6 servings.

Steak Diane

3 tablespoons chopped scallions
3 tablespoons vegetable oil
3 tablespoons finely chopped chives
3 tablespoons finely chopped parsley
1 tablespoon Worcestershire sauce
½ teaspoon salt
¼ teaspoon pepper
4 beef steaks, fillets, or rib-eye steaks
¼ cup brandy, warmed

Sauté scallions in 1 tablespoon hot vegetable oil a minute or two. Add chives, parsley, Worcestershire sauce, salt, and pepper.

In another frypan sauté steaks with remaining 2 tablespoons hot vegetable oil until done. (Time depends on thickness of steak.) Top each steak with some of scallion mixture.

Flame with warmed brandy until alcohol content is completely burned. Spoon pan juices over the steaks; serve. Makes 4 servings.

Steak au Poivre (Pepper Steak)

2 tablespoons black peppercorns
4 pieces fillet steak, 1 inch thick
4 tablespoons butter
2 teaspoons oil
¾ cup dry white wine
2 teaspoons brandy or dry sherry
2 teaspoons butter

Coarsely crush peppercorns with rolling pin or mortar and pestle. Press crushed peppercorns into fillets on both sides. (Add more crushed pepper if needed.) Allow steaks to stand for 1 hour to absorb flavor.

Heat 4 tablespoons butter and oil in pan; add steaks. Cook quickly on both sides to seal in the juices. Continue cooking until done to your preference (about 10 minutes for medium steak). Remove steaks to hot serving plate.

Stir wine and brandy into same pan; bring to boil, scraping pan. Remove from heat; stir in 2 teaspoons butter. Pour over steaks. Makes 4 servings.

Mushroom-Onion Lamb

3 pounds boned lamb
  shoulder
4 carrots
2 14-ounce cans chicken
  broth
Salt to taste
1 pound medium onions,
  peeled

1 pound medium
  mushrooms, stems
  removed
¼ cup butter
½ cup flour
2 egg yolks
½ cup whipping cream
2 teaspoons lemon juice
1 tablespoon finely
  chopped parsley

Trim excess fat from lamb; cut lamb into ½-inch cubes. Peel carrots; quarter lengthwise; cut quarters in half. Place lamb in Dutch oven; arrange carrots around lamb. Cover with broth; season with salt. Bring to boil over high heat, removing any scum. Turn into large casserole; cover. Bake in preheated 350°F oven 1 hour or until lamb is tender. Drain broth into 3-quart saucepan. Keep lamb mixture warm. Place onions in broth; cook until almost tender. Add mushrooms; cook 7 minutes longer. Remove onions and mushrooms; keep warm with lamb mixture. Strain broth; set aside. Melt butter in medium saucepan. Add flour; cook, stirring constantly, to make light-brown *roux*. Add broth gradually, stirring well after each addition; cook until smooth and thick.

Combine egg yolks and cream, mixing well. Stir small amount of broth mixture into egg mixture; slowly add egg mixture to broth mixture, stirring constantly. Place over very low heat until heated through and thickened, stirring constantly. Stir in lemon juice. Arrange lamb and vegetables on heated platter; pour sauce over all. Sprinkle with parsley; garnish with triangular-shaped croutons. Serve immediately. Makes 8 servings.

Orange Pork Chops

4 pork loin chops
1 clove garlic, crushed
½ teaspoon thyme
1 teaspoon salt
¼ teaspoon pepper
1 cup orange juice
2 tablespoons thinly
   sliced orange rind
4 tablespoons oil

2 tablespoons butter
1 onion, chopped
1 carrot, diced
1 stick celery, chopped
½ cup chicken stock
½ cup dry white wine
2 tablespoons chopped
   parsley

Dredge chops thoroughly with garlic, thyme, salt, and pepper.

Combine orange juice and rind in pot; bring to boil. Remove from heat; pour over chops. Allow chops to marinate several hours or overnight. Drain chops, reserving orange marinade.

Melt butter in frying pan. Add onion, carrot, and celery; sauté until carrot is tender and onion golden brown. Remove mixture from heat. Place vegetables in baking dish; cover vegetables with chops.

Combine reserved marinade, chicken stock, and wine; pour over chops and vegetables. Cover. Bake at 400°F for 40 minutes or until chops are tender.

Garnish chops with parsley; serve piping hot. Makes 4 servings.

Veal with Mushrooms

1½ pounds veal steaks
Flour for dredging meat
1 teaspoon salt
¼ teaspoon pepper
3 teaspoons flour
½ cup beef stock
½ cup cream
2 ounces mushrooms, sliced
1 tablespoon lemon juice

Pound veal steaks tender; dredge with flour seasoned with salt and pepper.

Melt butter in pan; fry veal on both sides until golden brown and cooked through. Remove to warming platter.

Stir 3 teaspoons flour into butter remaining in pan. Gradually add stock; continue stirring until sauce boils. Remove from flame; add cream.

In separate pan cook sliced mushrooms with lemon juice. When moisture has evaporated, remove from heat; place over veal steaks.

Cover steaks with sauce; serve at once. Makes 4 servings.

Paupiettes (Veal Rolls in Sauce)

4 veal scallops or cutlets
½ pound ham, finely diced
1 clove garlic, pressed
½ teaspoon marjoram
½ teaspoon rosemary
Salt and pepper to taste
5 tablespoons butter
1 tablespoon olive oil
1 large carrot, finely chopped
1 large onion, finely chopped
½ cup dry white wine
½ cup beef broth
½ teaspoon thyme
1 bay leaf
4 parsley stalks
1 tablespoon all-purpose flour

Pound scallops; trim into uniform rectangles. Mince scallop trimmings. Combine trimmings, ham, garlic, marjoram, rosemary, salt, and pepper; spread evenly over scallops. Roll scallops as for jelly roll; tie with string.

Melt 4 tablespoons butter with oil in frypan. Add carrot and onion; cook until golden, stirring frequently. Stir in wine and broth; add thyme, bay leaf, parsley stalks, salt, and pepper. Stir to mix well; pour into baking dish. Place veal rolls in sauce; cover. Bake in preheated 350°F oven, one shelf below center, 1 hour and 30 minutes. Remove casserole from oven; lift out veal rolls to serving dish. Remove string; keep veal rolls warm. Remove bay leaf and parsley stalks from sauce; pour sauce into blender container. Process sauce until pureed.

Melt 1 tablespoon butter in saucepan; stir in flour to make a smooth paste. Pour in sauce, stirring constantly; bring to boil. Reduce heat; simmer until sauce thickens.

Pour sauce over veal; garnish with finely chopped parsley. Serve with boiled new potatoes or rice. Makes 4 servings.

Coq au Vin

¼ pound butter
12 tiny onions
¼ pound bacon strips, cut into 1-inch pieces
4 pounds cut-up chicken pieces
½ pound mushrooms, sliced
1 clove garlic, crushed
½ cup flour
2½ cups chicken stock
⅓ cup brandy
1½ cups red wine
¼ teaspoon thyme
½ teaspoon mixed herbs
1 bay leaf
Salt and pepper to taste

Heat 4 tablespoons butter in heavy, shallow pan. Add onions and bacon; cook until onions are lightly browned. Remove from pan. Add chicken pieces to pan drippings; cook until well-browned on all sides. Set aside. Add mushrooms and garlic to pan; cook until mushrooms are wilted. Remove from pan.

Add remaining butter to pan drippings. Gradually stir in flour until golden brown. Remove from heat; gradually add chicken stock. Blend well. Return to heat; stir until sauce thickens. Add brandy, wine, thyme, herbs, and bay leaf.

Transfer chicken, vegetables, and sauce to deep pan. Cover; bring to boil. Reduce heat; simmer for 30 minutes. Season with salt and pepper. Remove bay leaf. This final step can be done, covered, in 400°F oven for 40 minutes or until chicken is tender to the fork.

Serve chicken with hot garlic bread and your favorite salad. Makes 6 servings.

Cold Chicken with Brandied Cream

This is a delicious, if filling, luncheon dish or cool summer dinner.

4 whole chicken breasts
½ cup mayonnaise
½ cup sour cream
1 tablespoon brandy
3 tablespoons cream
Salt and pepper to taste
Black grapes for garnish

Boned breasts are preferred and should be cooked ahead, halved, then chilled, keeping breast meat in one piece.

Mix mayonnaise, sour cream, and brandy in bowl, gradually adding cream to make a good coating consistency. Extra cream may be needed. Season sauce with salt and pepper to taste.

Place each chicken portion on bed of lettuce; spoon cream mixture over it. Refrigerate until ready to serve.

Garnish with grapes, if desired. Makes 4 servings.

Chicken Croquettes

2½ pounds chicken breasts
4 tablespoons butter
2 tablespoons flour
2 teaspoons unflavored gelatin
½ cup cream
1 teaspoon salt
¼ teaspoon pepper
2 tablespoons chopped parsley
½ teaspoon dry mustard
Pinch of cayenne
2 eggs
¼ cup milk
Packaged dry bread crumbs
Oil for deep frying

Steam or boil chicken until tender, setting aside stock in which it is cooked. Remove skin and bones from chicken; chop chicken meat into small pieces.

Heat butter in pan; gradually stir in flour. When well- blended, about 1 minute, remove from heat.

Stir gelatin into 1 cup hot chicken stock. When dissolved, add to flour mixture. Add cream; stir until smoothly blended. Return to heat; bring to boil. When thickened, add salt, pepper, parsley, mustard, and cayenne. Simmer just 2 minutes. Remove from heat; add chicken. When well- mixed, spread out on platter; refrigerate for 1 hour, until mixture is firm and set. With wet hands, shape mixture by tablespoonfuls into croquettes. Roll in dry bread crumbs. Dip into combined beaten eggs and milk. Roll again in bread crumbs. If you prefer a thicker crust, repeat egg and bread crumbs once more. Refrigerate at least 1 hour.

Heat oil for deep frying; place rolls into oil. Cook until golden brown; drain on paper. Croquettes may be kept in a warming oven until ready to serve. Makes 4 to 6 servings.

Jellied Chicken

3 pounds chicken parts, jointed	1 bay leaf
3 cups cold water	1 onion, chopped
3 small carrots, sliced	2 tablespoons chopped parsley
3 stalks celery, diced	1 tablespoon unflavored gelatin
1 teaspoon salt	1 tablespoon water
¼ teaspoon pepper	

Joint chicken. Prepare vegetables.

Place all ingredients except gelatin and 1 tablespoon water into large pot. Cover; simmer gently until chicken is all cooked, about 40 minutes. Remove from heat. Drain chicken and vegetables, reserving liquid. Remove chicken meat from bones; cut into cubes. Arrange half of cooked vegetables on greased tin. Place chopped chicken next; make final layer more vegetables.

Dissolve gelatin in 1 tablespoon water. Add to 2 cups of hot, strained chicken stock. Gently pour mixture over chicken and vegetables; refrigerate until set.

Unmold jellied chicken onto bed of shredded lettuce. Makes 4 to 6 servings.

Orange Chestnut Chicken

1 3-pound chicken	1 teaspoon sugar
6 tablespoons butter	1 teaspoon salt
1 cup orange juice	¼ teaspoon pepper
½ cup chicken stock	1 tablespoon cornstarch

Fill cavity and neck end of chicken with stuffing. Secure openings with skewers.

Melt butter in baking dish. Add chicken; brush with melted butter. Bake in moderate oven, basting occasionally with pan juices, 1½ hours or until chicken is tender. Remove chicken from baking dish; keep warm. Combine rest of ingredients; add to pan juices. Stir over moderate heat until sauce thickens. Reduce heat; simmer 3 minutes. Serve sauce separately in gravy boat. Makes 4 servings.

Chestnut Stuffing

4 tablespoons butter	1 8-ounce can
¼ cup chopped	unsweetened chestnut
mushrooms	puree
4 shallots, chopped	2 cups bread crumbs
1 tablespoon sweet	½ teaspoon thyme
sherry	Salt and pepper to taste

Heat butter in pan. Add mushrooms and shallots; sauté for 3 minutes. Remove from heat. Add sherry; mix well. Combine other ingredients; stir until well-mixed.

Chicken with Mushrooms

1 3-pound chicken	**½ teaspoon salt**
8 slices bacon	**¼ cup flour**
½ pound fresh mushrooms, chopped	**¾ cup chicken stock**
Pepper to taste	**¼ cup dry white wine**
½ cup butter	**½ cup whipping cream**

Preheat oven to 400°F.

Skin chicken; cut into 2 legs, 2 thighs, and 4 breast pieces. Lay each chicken piece on a bacon slice; sprinkle half the mushrooms over chicken. Season each portion with pepper. Roll bacon around chicken; secure with toothpicks.

Grease shallow baking dish with ¼ cup butter. Place bacon-wrapped chicken portions in baking dish; dot with small pieces of remaining butter. Sprinkle with salt. Cover. Bake on middle shelf 1 hour, basting occasionally. Remove cover; bake 15 minutes longer or until bacon is brown. Put chicken portions on heated serving dish; cover. Keep warm.

Drain liquid from baking dish into small saucepan. This should measure about ½ cup.

Place flour in small bowl; add enough stock to make a smooth paste.

Bring liquid in saucepan to boil; stir in flour paste. Gradually add remaining stock, stirring constantly. Stir in wine and cream. Cook and stir until thick and smooth.

Remove cover from serving dish; pour sauce over chicken. Makes 4 to 6 servings.

Chicken Provençal

3 pounds chicken, cut into serving pieces
¾ cup flour
1 teaspoon salt
¼ teaspoon pepper
¼ pound butter
1 onion, chopped fine
1 clove garlic, crushed
½ cup dry sherry
1 15-ounce can tomato puree
Black olives and chopped parsley for garnish

Roll chicken pieces in flour seasoned with salt and pepper.

Heat butter in frypan; sauté chicken pieces until golden on all sides. Transfer to casserole.

Add onion and garlic to butter remaining in frypan. Cook slowly until soft. Add sherry; boil for 1 minute. Add tomato puree; stir until mixture comes to boil. Pour over chicken. Bake, covered, in moderate (400°F) oven 1 hour.

Garnish chicken with olives and parsley; serve. Makes 4 servings.

Chicken in Red Wine

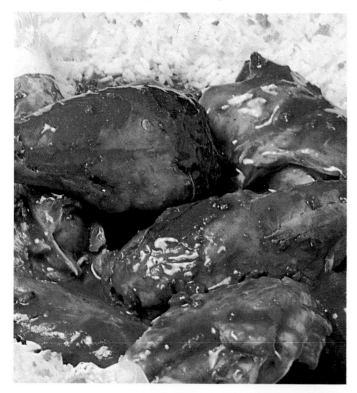

4 whole chicken legs
2 teaspoons salt
1 teaspoon paprika
¼ teaspoon thyme
1 bay leaf
¾ cup dry red wine
1 cup water
½ cup tomato juice
1 teaspoon salt
¼ teaspoon pepper
Chopped parsley for garnish

Separate chicken into thighs and drumsticks, or keep whole, according to your preference.

Mix salt and paprika; rub well into chicken pieces. Broil chicken until browned evenly on both sides. Remove from broiler. Place in ovenproof dish. Add thyme, bay leaf, wine, and water. Cover; put in 400°F oven 1 hour or until chicken is tender. Place chicken on warming dish.

Pour juices into small pan. Add tomato juice, salt, and pepper; heat until all flavors blend.

Pour sauce over chicken; garnish with parsley. Serve at once. Makes 4 servings.

Chicken Tourangelle

1 4-pound stewing chicken
2 large onions, quartered
2 cups chicken stock
6 to 8 medium mushrooms
½ cup dry white wine
½ cup whipping cream
Salt and freshly ground pepper to taste
Grated rind of ½ orange
2 cups mashed potatoes
2 tablespoons toasted sliced almonds

Place chicken, onions, and stock in roasting pan; cover. Bake in preheated 325°F oven 2 hours or until chicken is tender. Remove chicken from roasting pan; cool until easily handled. Remove skin and bones from chicken; cut chicken into serving pieces. Arrange on heated platter; keep warm.

Cut stems from mushrooms; cut caps in half. Add mushroom caps and stems to liquid in roasting pan; bring to boil over high heat. Boil until liquid is reduced to 2 cups. Stir in wine and cream; boil until reduced to 2 cups liquid. Season with salt and pepper; stir in orange rind. Pour sauce over chicken.

Place mashed potatoes in pastry bag with large writing tube affixed; pipe around chicken mixture. Sprinkle potato mixture with almonds. Makes 6 servings.

Chicken Vol-au-Vent

2 whole chicken breasts
4 tablespoons butter
3 tablespoons flour
1 cup chicken stock
¾ cup cream
Salt and pepper to taste
2 ounces grated cheddar
  cheese
1 7-ounce can champignons
  (small mushrooms)

3 shallots, chopped
1 tablespoon chopped
  parsley
2 teaspoons dry sherry
1½ teaspoons prepared
  mustard
4 patty-shell cases
  (vol-au-vents)

Cook chicken breasts in boiling water until meat is tender.
Reserve stock. Remove bones and skin; cut meat into 1-inch
pieces.

Melt butter in pan; stir in flour. Remove from heat. Gradually
add chicken stock and cream, stirring until combined. Return to
heat; allow sauce to thicken. Season with salt and pepper; simmer for 2 minutes more. Add grated cheese, sliced mushrooms,
shallots, parsley, sherry, and mustard. Stir until cheese has
melted. Add chicken pieces; heat through over low flame.

Warm the patty shells in moderate (350°F) oven until hot.
Spoon chicken mixture into patty shells. Garnish with chopped
parsley or dill if desired. Makes 4 servings.

Baked Clams in Mornay Sauce

1 pint shucked clams
Dry white wine
1 recipe Basic Mornay Sauce (see Index)
2 tablespoons fine dry bread crumbs
1 tablespoon freshly grated Parmesan cheese
2 teaspoons chopped parsley
2 teaspoons chopped chives
Butter

Mince clams; place in saucepan. Add just enough wine to cover. Simmer about 5 minutes or until wine has evaporated. Combine clams and sauce; mix well. Spoon clam mixture into scallop shells or individual baking dishes.

Blend bread crumbs, cheese, parsley, and chives. Sprinkle over clam mixture; dot with butter. Place shells on baking sheet. Bake in preheated 350°F oven, 1 rack above center, 15 minutes. Makes 8 servings.

Fried Dabs with Tartar Sauce

4 whole dabs or small flounder fillets
All-purpose flour
2 eggs, beaten
Fine dry bread crumbs
2 hard-boiled eggs, finely chopped
1 tablespoon freshly minced parsley
1 cup tartar sauce

Wash dabs; pat dry. Coat dabs with flour, shaking off any excess; dip into beaten eggs. Coat generously with bread crumbs, patting crumbs into egg coating firmly. Fry dabs in deep fat at 375°F until brown on both sides. Drain on paper toweling; arrange on heated serving platter. Sprinkle with eggs, then parsley.

Serve dabs with the sauce and French bread. Makes 4 servings.

Lenten Mackerel

4 medium tomatoes, skinned
1 small onion, thinly sliced
4 peppercorns
2 strips lemon peel
4 thick mackerel or snapper steaks
Leaves of 4 small sprigs thyme
Leaves of 2 sprigs fennel
Salt to taste
½ cup fish stock
½ cup dry white wine

Slice tomatoes. Arrange tomato and onion slices in well- buttered, shallow baking pan. Add peppercorns and lemon peel. Arrange mackerel steaks over tomato mixture. Sprinkle with thyme and fennel leaves; season with salt. Pour stock and wine into baking pan; cover. Bake in preheated 325°F oven 20 to 25 minutes or until mackerel flakes easily when pierced with a fork. One-half teaspoon powdered thyme and 1 teaspoon dried fennel may be substituted for thyme and fennel leaves. Makes 4 servings.

Salmon Quiche

Pastry

1 cup flour
Pinch of salt
6 tablespoons butter
1 egg yolk

1 tablespoon lemon juice
1 or 2 teaspoons water, if
needed

Sift flour and salt into bowl. Cut in butter until mixture resembles fine bread crumbs. Mix to firm dough with egg yolk and lemon juice, adding water if needed. Turn pastry onto lightly floured board; knead lightly. Roll to line base and sides of 9-inch quiche pan, approximately a 10-inch circle.

Salmon Quiche Filling

1 8-ounce can red salmon
4 strips bacon, diced
1½ cups cream
3 eggs
1 teaspoon salt
¼ teaspoon pepper

½ teaspoon paprika
2 tablespoons chopped
parsley
1 tablespoon grated
Parmesan cheese

Drain salmon, reserving liquid. Remove bones; flake salmon lightly. Dice bacon; fry gently until crisp. Drain well.

Beat together cream, eggs, salt, pepper, paprika, parsley, cheese, and reserved salmon liquid.

Place salmon evenly in base of pastry shell; sprinkle bacon over. Gently pour in egg mixture. Bake at 450°F 10 minutes. Reduce heat to 350°F; cook 30 minutes more or until set in center. Slice; serve. Makes 4 to 6 servings.

Coquilles Saint Jacques

1½ cups sauterne
2 pounds fresh scallops
½ pound medium
   mushrooms, sliced
6 green onions, finely
   chopped
6 tablespoons butter
3 tablespoons water
1 tablespoon finely
   chopped parsley

1 tablespoon lemon juice
¼ cup all-purpose flour
2 egg yolks
¼ cup whipping cream
½ teaspoon salt
1/8 teaspoon freshly
   ground pepper
2 cups mashed potatoes

Bring sauterne to boil in medium-size saucepan; add scallops.
Reduce heat; simmer 3 minutes or until scallops are tender.
Drain; set aside. Reserve broth. Combine mushrooms, onions, 2
tablespoons butter, water, parsley, and lemon juice in saucepan. Cover; simmer about 10 minutes, stirring occasionally.
Melt remaining butter in saucepan. Stir in flour; cook, stirring
constantly, until lightly browned. Stir in reserved broth slowly;
cook, stirring constantly, until thickened and smooth. Remove
from heat. Combine egg yolks and cream; beat well. Add part
of hot sauce to egg mixture very slowly, beating constantly with
whisk. Beat egg mixture into remaining sauce. Season with salt
and pepper. Stir in mushroom mixture, then scallops. Spoon
evenly into 8 scallop shells or small ramekins. Pipe mashed
potatoes around shells. Place shells in jelly-roll pan. Bake in
preheated 400°F oven 15 to 20 minutes or until potatoes are
lightly browned. Serve immediately. Makes 8 servings.

Shrimp-Filled Brioche

½ pound fresh shrimp
½ cup minced celery
1 small cucumber, peeled and diced
½ cup cooked green peas
½ cup mayonnaise
2 teaspoons lemon juice
3 or 4 drops hot sauce
Salt and pepper to taste
1 brioche, hollowed-out

Cook and clean shrimp; chill. Combine shrimp, celery, cucumber, and peas in mixing bowl.

Combine mayonnaise, lemon juice, and hot sauce. Add shrimp mixture; toss carefully. Season with salt and pepper; pack into brioche shell. Wrap tightly in foil; refrigerate until ready to serve. Makes 4 servings.

Shrimp and Cream-Cheese Crepes

1 pound fresh shrimp
10 cooked crepes (made ahead and kept warm)
1 8-ounce package cream cheese, softened
1 cup half-and-half cream
Salt and pepper to taste
Melted butter
Freshly grated Parmesan cheese

Cook and clean shrimp; set aside.

Prepare crepes of your favorite recipe; set aside to keep warm.

Place cream cheese in heavy saucepan; stir in half the cream. Cook over low heat until smooth, stirring constantly. Reserve ⅓ of shrimp for garnish; add remaining shrimp to cream-cheese mixture; cook until heated through, stirring constantly. Season with salt and pepper. Spread cream-cheese mixture over half of each crepe; fold other half over top. Arrange crepes in buttered baking dish. Pour remaining ½ cup cream around crepes; drizzle tops with melted butter. Sprinkle generously with Parmesan cheese. Bake in preheated 450°F oven until brown and bubbly. Arrange reserved shrimp over crepes. Serve immediately. Makes 5 servings.

Herb-Stuffed Trout with Sauce

6 dressed fresh trout
2 bay leaves, halved
1 small shallot, thinly
  sliced
4 peppercorns
2 or 3 sprigs parsley
1 teaspoon salt
½ cup wine vinegar
½ cup water
1½ cups soft bread
  crumbs

1 egg, beaten
2 tablespoons freshly
  minced parsley
1 tablespoon chopped
  chives
Salt and pepper to taste
Melted butter
1 tablespoon capers
1 small lemon, cut into
  sections

Remove heads and tails from trout; bone without cutting in half. Place in shallow glass container. Combine bay leaves, shallot, peppercorns, parsley, and 1 teaspoon salt; sprinkle over trout. Mix vinegar and water; pour over trout. Marinate in refrigerator overnight. Drain; reserve marinade.

Combine crumbs, egg, 1 tablespoon parsley, chives, and salt and pepper to taste in bowl; mix well. Stuff trout cavities with dressing; brush trout with melted butter. Arrange trout in shallow baking dish; cover lightly with aluminum foil. Bake in preheated 375°F oven about 20 minutes or until trout flakes easily.

Strain reserved marinade; place in small saucepan. Stir in capers, remaining parsley, lemon sections, and marinade mixture. Heat through. Arrange trout on serving dish; pour sauce over; serve hot. Makes 6 servings.

Lemon Trout with Parsley Jelly

4 fresh dressed trout
½ cup dry white wine
2 tablespoons vegetable
  oil
1 small onion, sliced
½ cup chopped green
  onions
½ bay leaf
½ teaspoon salt

½ teaspoon thyme
3 peppercorns
Juice of 1 lemon
3 cups fish stock
1 tablespoon butter
2 envelopes unflavored
  gelatin
3 tablespoons minced
  parsley

Place trout in buttered, shallow baking dish.

Combine wine, oil, onion slices, green onions, bay leaf, salt, thyme, peppercorns, lemon juice, fish stock, and butter in medium-size saucepan; bring to boil. Simmer for 15 minutes. Strain; pour over trout. Cover with aluminum foil. Bake in preheated 350°F oven about 20 minutes or until trout flakes easily when pierced with a fork. Remove baking dish from oven; lift out trout. Remove skins from just below heads to just above tails, then place trout in deep platter.

Soften gelatin in ½ cup cold water; stir into hot liquid in baking dish until dissolved. Add parsley; mix well. Pour over trout. Cool; chill until firm. Garnish with canelled lemon slices. Makes 4 servings.

Bouillabaisse

1 pound fish fillets
1 pound cooked prawns
1 pound scallops
2 tablespoons butter
1 medium onion, finely chopped
2 sticks celery, finely diced
1 small green pepper, finely diced
1 clove garlic, crushed

1 cup dry white wine
1 teaspoon Worcestershire sauce
1 teaspoon sugar
1 15-ounce can whole tomatoes, mashed
2 cups fish stock or water
3 tablespoons chopped parsley

Cut boned fillets into bite-size pieces. Shell and devein prawns. Wash and trim scallops.

Melt butter. Sauté onion, celery, green pepper, and garlic 3 minutes.

Combine wine, Worcestershire sauce, sugar, and tomatoes with their liquid. Add tomato mixture and fish stock to pan; bring to boil. Simmer gently 5 minutes. Mash tomatoes to make a puree. Add fish pieces and scallops; cook 5 to 7 minutes more, until fish is tender. Stir in prawns and parsley; simmer 3 minutes more. Serve at once, piping hot. Makes 4 to 6 servings.

Broccoli Casserole

1 package frozen broccoli
1¼ cups milk
3 eggs, lightly beaten
½ teaspoon salt
½ teaspoon nutmeg
½ cup grated cheese

Preheat oven to 350°F.

Cook broccoli in small amount of boiling water 3 minutes; drain.

Pour milk into small saucepan; bring to boil. Cool to lukewarm.

Mix eggs with salt and nutmeg. Add milk and cheese, beating constantly. Pour into greased baking dish; add broccoli. Bake for 30 to 40 minutes or until knife inserted in center comes out clean. Must be served hot. Makes 3 to 4 servings.

Stuffed Artichokes

4 artichokes
2 lemons

2 cups chicken stock

Remove stalk from artichoke, cutting across base with sharp knife. Slice ½ inch off top leaves. Trim outer leaves with scissors, ½ inch from tips. Rinse under cold water. Cut lemon into slices ½ inch thick. Place lemon and artichokes in chicken stock that has come to boil. Reduce heat; simmer for 15 minutes, until leaves can be pulled out easily. Remove from pan; turn upside down to drain.

Anchovy Filling

4 tablespoons butter
1 medium onion, chopped
1 clove garlic, crushed
2½ cups bread crumbs
1 2-ounce can anchovy fillets, drained, finely chopped
3 tablespoons chopped parsley

½ teaspoon salt
Dash of pepper

1 cup sour cream
1 tablespoon grated onion
1 teaspoon grated lemon rind
½ cup grated Parmesan cheese

Melt butter in frypan. Add chopped onion and garlic; sauté until onion is tender. Add 2 cups bread crumbs, stirring until bread crumbs are golden brown. Remove from heat. Add anchovy fillets, parsley, salt, and pepper.

Pull leaves gently away from artichoke tops so that centers show. Spoon bread-crumb mixture into openings.

Combine sour cream, grated onion, and lemon rind; spoon over artichokes. Top with ½ cup crumbs and cheese. Stand artichokes in 1 inch water in baking dish. Bake in 400°F oven 15 minutes or until tops are golden brown. Makes 4 servings.

Cauliflower with Mornay Sauce

1 large head cauliflower
Freshly grated bread crumbs
⅓ cup melted butter
Basic Mornay Sauce

Wash and trim cauliflower, then separate into florets. Place in vegetable steamer; steam until tender. Arrange around edge of baking dish. Sprinkle liberally with bread crumbs. Drizzle butter over bread crumbs. Spoon Mornay Sauce into center of baking dish. Broil until crumbs are lightly browned. Makes 4 to 6 servings.

Basic Mornay Sauce

1 cup white sauce
2 tablespoons butter
1 cup grated Parmesan cheese

Prepare white sauce; remove from heat.

Cut butter into small pieces. Stir Parmesan cheese and butter into white sauce, beating with wooden spoon until butter is melted. Amount of salt in white sauce may be decreased if desired, because Parmesan cheese sometimes imparts a salty flavor.

Mushroom Soufflé

**2 cups finely chopped
  fresh mushrooms**
½ cup vermouth
¾ cup milk
3 tablespoons butter
**3 tablespoons all-purpose
  flour**
¾ teaspoon salt
**¼ teaspoon white
  pepper**
5 eggs, separated

Combine mushrooms and vermouth in small saucepan. Add milk; bring to boil. Reduce heat; simmer for 15 minutes.

Melt butter in saucepan; stir in flour. Cook, stirring constantly, until golden. Stir in mushroom mixture; cook, stirring constantly, about 3 minutes or until thick. Remove from heat. Season with salt and pepper.

Beat egg yolks with fork until light and lemon-colored. Pour egg yolks slowly into mushroom mixture, beating vigorously with wooden spoon. Bring just to boiling point, but do not boil. Remove from heat; stir constantly several minutes or until cooled.

Beat egg whites until stiff but not dry. Fold about ⅓ of egg whites thoroughly into mushroom mixture; add remaining egg whites. Fold in lightly but thoroughly. Turn into 7- inch buttered and floured soufflé dish. Bake in preheated 350°F oven 35 minutes or until puffed, browned, and firm in center. Makes 4 servings.

Fried Onion Rings

4 to 6 onions
1 cup milk
1 cup flour
1 egg
1 teaspoon salt
¼ teaspoon pepper
Oil for deep frying

Peel onions; slice thin. Separate into individual rings; put into bowl. Pour milk over onions; allow to stand 1 hour. Drain milk, reserving it for use in batter.

Sift flour into bowl. Add egg, reserved milk, salt, and pepper. Beat well to form very smooth batter.

Dip each onion ring into batter; deep fry in hot oil, a few rings at a time. When onion rings are crisp and golden brown, drain them; sprinkle with salt. Keep in warming oven until all onion rings are ready to serve. Makes 4 to 6 servings.

Pommes Anna

2 pounds potatoes
½ cup melted butter
¼ cup grated onion
Salt and white pepper to taste

Peel potatoes; cut into paper-thin slices.

Brush bottom and sides of 6½ x 3-inch soufflé dish generously with butter. Arrange potatoes, overlapping slices, around sides of soufflé dish to form a firm wall; place an overlapping layer of potatoes in bottom of dish to cover. Brush lightly with butter; sprinkle lightly with onion, salt, and pepper. Repeat layers until all ingredients are used; cover lightly with foil. Bake in preheated 400°F oven 30 minutes. Remove foil; bake 30 minutes longer or until top is well-browned.

Unmold potatoes onto heated serving platter. Makes 6 to 8 servings.

Crisp Potato Balls

2 pounds potatoes,
  mashed
4 tablespoons butter
3 strips bacon, finely
  chopped
4 shallots, chopped
4 ounces grated cheddar
  cheese

1 ounce grated Parmesan
  cheese
1 teaspoon salt
¼ teaspoon pepper
2 eggs, beaten
½ cup milk
2 cups bread crumbs
Oil for deep frying

If you do not have leftover mashed potatoes, cook 2 pounds potatoes and mash them as usual.

Heat butter in pan; add bacon. Fry until crisp. Add bacon and butter mixture to mashed potatoes. Add shallots, grated cheeses, salt, and pepper. Mix well. Take tablespoons of potato mixture and roll into balls with floured hands.

Combine beaten eggs and milk. Coat each potato ball with egg mixture; roll balls in bread crumbs. Repeat egg and bread crumbing to give a firm coating. Deep fry a few balls at a time in hot oil until golden brown and crisp. Drain well; keep balls warm until all are fried. Serve hot. Makes 4 to 6 servings.

Spinach Florentine

2 10-ounce packages frozen spinach
1 cup cooked rice
4 ounces grated cheddar cheese
4 eggs
½ cup cream
¼ teaspoon nutmeg
1 teaspoon salt
¼ teaspoon pepper
¼ cup milk
1 ounce grated Parmesan cheese

Allow frozen spinach to thaw completely. Drain well. Place half the spinach into large, well-greased casserole. Cover with cooked rice. Sprinkle with ¾ of grated cheddar cheese. Top evenly with remaining spinach.

Beat together eggs, cream, nutmeg, salt, and pepper.

Heat milk almost to boiling. Gently stir warm milk into egg mixture. When blended, pour over spinach. Top with remaining cheeses. Bake in moderately slow (350°F) oven 30 to 35 minutes or until top is set and golden brown. Makes 4 to 6 servings.

Tomato Flan

Pastry

1 tablespoon butter	1 egg yolk, lightly beaten
1 cup flour	1 tablespoon lemon juice
Pinch of salt	

In bowl cut butter into combined flour and salt. When mixture resembles fine bread crumbs, add egg yolk and lemon juice. Add 1 to 2 teaspoons water if needed to make dough hold together. Turn pastry onto lightly floured surface; roll to 10-inch circle (will fit bottom and sides of 9-inch pie pan). Line pan with pastry; refrigerate 1 hour.

Tomato Filling

2 medium onions, chopped fine	1 teaspoon sugar
3 sticks celery, diced	2 eggs
2 tablespoons butter	1 cup cream
1 pound tomatoes, peeled and chopped	1 tablespoon grated Parmesan cheese
1 teaspoon salt	¼ teaspoon Worcestershire sauce
¼ teaspoon pepper	Pinch of nutmeg
1 clove garlic, crushed	

Sauté onion and celery in melted butter until onion is transparent. Add tomatoes, salt, pepper, garlic, and sugar; bring to boil. Reduce heat; simmer until mixture has thickened, about 30 minutes. Allow to cool. Combine eggs, cream, cheese, Worcestershire sauce, and nutmeg; mix well. Spoon cool Tomato Filling into pastry shell; gently pour over egg mixture. Bake 10 minutes at 425°F. Reduce heat to 350°F; bake 20 minutes more or until mixture is set in center. Makes 6 servings.

Savory Bread Omelet

3 eggs
Salt and pepper to taste
1½ teaspoons finely chopped fresh parsley
1 tablespoon butter
½ cup fried croutons
2 tablespoons grated Parmesan cheese

Beat eggs lightly with fork. Season with salt and pepper; add parsley. Beat again.

Melt butter in 9-inch omelet pan until butter just begins to brown around edge. Add egg mixture; reduce heat. Lift around edge with fork or spatula; tilt pan to allow egg to run underneath. Cook until browned and set on bottom but top is still moist. Sprinkle croutons to within 1 inch of edge; sprinkle with 1 tablespoon cheese. Flip over; slide onto heated plate. Sprinkle with remaining cheese. Serve immediately. Makes 1 to 2 servings.

Omelet with Chicken Livers

2 tablespoons butter
½ cup finely chopped onions
½ pound chicken livers, quartered
½ cup beef consommé
¼ cup sherry
½ cup half-and-half cream
½ teaspoon salt
Pepper to taste
1 French omelet
Fresh parsley, finely chopped

Melt butter in medium-size saucepan over medium heat. Add onions and livers; cook, stirring occasionally, until browned. Add consommé and sherry. Simmer about 10 minutes or until livers are tender. Remove livers with slotted spoon; keep them warm.

Add cream to pan juices slowly, stirring constantly. Increase heat; cook until sauce is thick and creamy. Season with salt and pepper.

Prepare French omelet in usual way; turn out onto heated platter. Pour sauce over omelet. Arrange livers over top; sprinkle with parsley. Serve at once. Makes 2 to 3 servings.

Shrimp Omelet

¼ cup chopped mushrooms	1 pound shrimp
1 teaspoon oil	8 eggs
6 shallots or spring onions, chopped	1 cup bean sprouts
2 stalks celery, chopped	1 teaspoon salt
	¼ teaspoon pepper
	1 tablespoon oil

Wash and chop mushrooms. Cook in hot oil until tender. Drain. Chop onions and celery fine. Shell, devein, and chop shrimp.

Beat eggs slightly. Add shrimp, shallots, celery, mushrooms, bean sprouts, salt, and pepper. Mix lightly.

Heat oil in large frypan. Pour in enough omelet mixture to make 5-inch omelet. Several individual omelets can cook at same time. When firm on one side, turn and cook other side. Stack finished omelets on warming plate while cooking rest of omelets. Serve with sauce spooned over. Makes 4 to 6 servings.

Sauce

1 cup chicken stock	1 tablespoon cornstarch
1 teaspoon sugar	¼ cup cold water
2 teaspoons soy sauce	

Combine stock, sugar, and soy sauce in saucepan; bring to boil.

Mix cornstarch with cold water; add to saucepan. Mix well, stirring until mixture boils and thickens.

Onion Pancakes

1 cup flour	1 egg, beaten
Pinch of salt	1¼ cups milk

Sift flour and salt into bowl; make well in center of dry ingredients. Combine egg and milk; gradually add to flour. Mix to smooth batter.

Heat griddle or frypan; grease lightly. Pour 2 or 3 tablespoons mixture into pan to form fairly large pancake. Loosen edges of pancake with knife; when lightly browned underneath and bubbles form in center, turn and brown other side. Repeat this process, making 1 pancake at a time until all batter is used, about 8 to 10 pancakes.

Onion Filling

6 tablespoons butter	Dash of pepper
3 large onions, finely chopped	½ teaspoon dry mustard
3 tablespoons flour	Pinch of nutmeg
1⅔ cups milk	8 ounces grated cheddar cheese
1 teaspoon salt	

Heat butter in pan; sauté onions until tender. Add flour; stir until well-mixed. Remove from heat. Gradually add milk; stir until combined. Return to heat; stir until sauce boils and thickens. Reduce heat; add salt, pepper, mustard, and nutmeg. Mix well; simmer 5 minutes, stirring occasionally.

Stack pancakes on ovenproof dish, layering each with onion sauce and some grated cheese. Top last pancake on stack with grated cheese only. Bake whole stack in hot (450°F) oven 10 minutes or until cheese is golden brown. Cut stack into wedges to serve. Makes about 4 servings.

Seafood Pancakes (Crepes)

⅓ cup flour	1 egg
Pinch of salt	⅓ cup milk

Sift flour and salt into bowl. Add egg. Gradually add milk; mix to smooth batter. Heat pan; grease well. Pour 2 to 3 tablespoons batter into pan. Cook slowly until batter is set and lightly browned underneath. Turn; brown second side. Makes 4 fairly large pancakes; set aside.

Seafood Filling

1 pound shrimp	½ cup cream
½ pound scallops	1 teaspoon salt
1 cup water	½ teaspoon pepper
½ cup dry white wine	3 shallots, chopped
1 small onion, chopped fine	Salt and pepper to taste
3 tablespoons flour	⅓ cup dry bread crumbs
6 tablespoons butter	2 ounces cheddar cheese, grated

Shell and devein shrimp, reserving shells. Clean scallops. Place reserved shells, water, wine, and onion in saucepan; bring to boil. Simmer, uncovered, 5 minutes. Drain; reserve stock. Return stock to pan. Add scallops; simmer 3 minutes. Drain; reserve stock. Stir flour and 4 tablespoons butter over low heat until combined. Remove from heat; add 1 cup stock and cream. Bring sauce to boil; stir until it thickens. Simmer 3 minutes. Gently sauté shallots in 2 tablespoons butter 1 minute. Add seafood; mix well. Add sauce; season with salt and pepper to taste.

Spoon filling down center of each pancake; roll up. Place on greased baking sheet; sprinkle with bread crumbs and cheese. Bake at 500°F for 5 minutes or until heated through. Makes 4 servings.

Cheese Soufflé

4 eggs, separated
¼ pound butter
4 tablespoons flour
1 teaspoon salt
¼ teaspoon pepper

¼ teaspoon dry mustard
1 cup milk
4 ounces cheddar
cheese, grated

Separate egg yolks from whites; set aside.

Melt butter in top of double boiler over hot water. Remove from heat. Stir in flour and seasonings until free of lumps and very smooth. Gradually stir in milk. Return to heat, again over hot water, stirring until mixture is thick and smooth. Remove from heat. Stir in grated cheese until cheese melts in hot mixture. Allow to cool slightly.

Beat egg yolks until pale and fluffy. Gradually fold yolks into cheese mixture.

Beat egg whites until soft peaks form. Add half the whites to sauce, folding through carefully. Fold in remaining whites. Pour soufflé into well-greased dish or individual molds. Bake at 425°F or until soufflé is set.

This soufflé may be kept uncovered in refrigerator overnight and baked the next day.

To freeze: Cover soufflé dish with aluminum foil to prevent hard skin forming. When ready to bake, remove foil; place in cold, unlit oven. Turn oven heat to 425°F; bake at least 40 minutes. Makes 4 to 6 servings.

Rum Babas

1 package active dry yeast
2 teaspoons sugar
¼ cup lukewarm milk
2 cups flour

Pinch of salt
3 eggs, well-beaten
2 tablespoons butter
3 tablespoons currants
¼ pound butter

Mix together yeast, 2 teaspoons sugar, and milk.

Sift flour with salt; make well in center. Add yeast mixture and well-beaten eggs. Dot surface with 2 tablespoons softened butter. Cover; put aside in warm place to rise (about 40 minutes to double in bulk). Then mix in currants and ¼ pound softened butter; knead well. Divide mixture into 8 well-greased ovenproof cups. Each cup will be ¾ full. Let rise 10 minutes more. Bake at 450°F for 15 minutes, until well-risen and golden. Drop into hot sauce, if desired; serve with cream. (Babas can be prepared in advance and reheated in hot sauce.) Makes 8 babas.

Apricot Rum Sauce

2 cups apricot nectar
2 cups sugar

1½ tablespoons lemon juice
¼ cup rum

Combine apricot nectar and 2 cups sugar in saucepan. Stir over low heat until sugar dissolves. Bring to boil; boil rapidly 5 minutes. Remove from heat; stir in lemon juice and rum.

Crème Caramel

Caramel

1 cup sugar
1 cup water

Place 1 cup sugar and water in shallow pan on medium heat. When sugar has dissolved, increase heat; boil rapidly until mixture turns deep golden brown. Do not stir, or mixture may crystallize. Immediately pour caramel into 8-inch- square baking pan. Be sure caramel coats sides and base of pan. Allow to cool completely. (Caramel melts again when baked with custard.)

Custard

3 cups milk
1 cup cream
6 eggs
1½ teaspoons vanilla

½ cup sugar
Whipped cream for garnish

Combine milk and cream in saucepan. Bring to scalding point; cool slightly. Beat eggs, vanilla, and ½ cup sugar together lightly. Gradually pour milk over egg mixture, stirring constantly. For a more velvety texture, strain once. Pour custard carefully into baking dish. Place baking dish in pan of hot water halfway up outside of baking dish. Bake at 350°F for 30 minutes or until custard is set. Cool; then refrigerate. When cold, turn out and cut into slices or squares. Garnish with whipped cream, if desired. Makes 4 to 6 servings.

Chocolate Crepes

2 tablespoons cocoa
1 cup sifted all-purpose flour
¼ cup sugar
¼ teaspoon salt
3 eggs
1 cup milk
½ teaspoon vanilla
2 tablespoons melted butter

Sift cocoa, flour, sugar, and salt together into medium-size mixing bowl.

Beat eggs with electric mixer at medium speed 5 minutes or until thick. Stir milk, vanilla, and butter into eggs. Blend egg mixture into flour mixture until smooth.

Make crepes as you normally do. Fold crepes into quarters; dust with confectioners' sugar. Top with sweetened whipped cream flavored with creme de cacao, if desired. Makes about 20 crepes.

Strawberry Liqueur Crepes

1 cup flour	2 eggs
Pinch of salt	1 cup milk

Put flour and salt in bowl, making a well in center. Add eggs and a little milk. Mix to smooth batter. Gradually add remaining milk. Allow batter to stand 30 minutes. Grease pan lightly. Pour 2 to 3 tablespoons batter into pan. When crepe is set and light golden brown underneath, turn it and cook other side. Set each crepe aside as finished until all are cooked.

Strawberry Sauce

1 quart strawberries	¼ cup brandy
1 teaspoon butter	½ cup orange juice
½ cup sugar	Whipped cream for
¼ of a lemon	garnish
2 tablespoons Grand Marnier	

Wash and hull strawberries. Set aside 8 berries for garnish. Melt butter in frying pan; add sugar. Push a fork through skin side of lemon wedge; stir sugar with lemon until sugar turns light golden brown. Remove from heat. Add Grand Marnier, brandy, and orange juice; stir until sugar is dissolved. Return to heat; simmer until liquid is reduced by half. Remove from heat. Stir strawberries lightly into mixture, coating all berries. Place some berries in center of each crepe; roll up crepes. Spoon some of sauce over rolled crepes; decorate each with whipped cream and reserved strawberries. Serve remaining sauce separately in a sauce boat. Other fruit in season may also be used in the same way. Makes 4 servings.

Chocolate Mousse

1 tablespoon gelatin
1½ cups water
¼ cup cocoa
¾ cup milk
2 eggs
½ cup sugar
½ teaspoon vanilla
1¼ cups heavy whipped cream
Whipped cream for garnish
Grated chocolate for garnish

Sprinkle gelatin over ½ cup water. Stir until dissolved.

Combine cocoa, remaining water, and milk in large saucepan. Bring to boil, stirring constantly. Remove from heat; add gelatin mixture. When dissolved, set aside to cool.

Beat together eggs and sugar until fluffy. Add to cooled cocoa mixture. Return to heat, stirring until just reaching boiling point. Remove from heat. Add vanilla; cool, stirring occasionally.

Whip heavy cream quite stiff. When cocoa mixture is cold, fold in whipped cream. Pour into serving bowl or individual dishes. Refrigerate until set. Garnish with extra whipped cream and grated chocolate. Makes 4 to 6 servings.

Strawberry Mousse

1 generous quart strawberries
⅓ cup powdered sugar
1 tablespoon gelatin
¼ cup water
1¼ cups heavy cream
2 tablespoons Grand Marnier
Extra whipped cream for topping

Wash and hull strawberries, reserving 6 large berries for decoration. Place strawberries in blender with sugar. Blend on medium speed until smooth.

Sprinkle gelatin over cold water; stir until combined. Stand gelatin over simmering water until it dissolves. Allow gelatin mixture to become cold but not to set. Add to strawberries in blender; blend on medium speed 1 minute.

Beat heavy cream until soft peaks form. Fold cream and Grand Marnier into strawberry mixture. Pour into individual serving glasses; refrigerate until set.

Top each serving glass with a portion of whipped cream and a reserved strawberry. Makes 6 servings.

Index